What is...

Truth?

Also by Darren J Nast

PONDER A PARADOX I
PONDER A PARADOX II
PONDER A PARADOX III

What is... Truth?

Darren J Nast

Victoria, B.C.
CANADA

FB: Ponder a Paradox community
www.ponderaparadox.com

What is... Truth?
First paperback Ponder a Paradox Publication Marchs 2012

Cover Photo/Design: Ponder a Paradox Publishing
Cover Design Assistant: Erik Pedersen
Author Photo: © Darren J Nast

Copyright © Darren J Nast, 2012
All rights reserved.

1. Philosophy   2. Spirituality   3. Title

Nast, Darren J, 1966 –

Printed in USA
ISBN #: 978-0-9876945-1-5

Without limiting copyright that is reserved above, no part of this publication may be reproduced, stored in or introduced into any retrieval system, or transmitted, by any form, by any means (electronic, mechanical, photocopying, recording or other), without the prior written consent of both the copyright owner and the publisher of this book. The uploading, scanning or distribution of this publication by the Internet or by any other form without the explicit written permission of the publisher is illegal and punishable by applicable laws. Please buy only authorized print and electronic versions, and do not engage in or encourage others in print or electronic piracy of copyright materials. Those who rely on the income from this publication appreciate your support of the rights of the author and publisher.

Special thanks to—

Dad, Mom, Drs. K & K Shahin, Erik and Peggy, Lally, the moss, and all connected, and many others.

For R & R

TABLE OF CONTENTS

Notice to Reader

Dear Reader

Chapter 1 What Is?	1
Chapter 2 Truth?	11
Chapter 3 Do I Experience Truth?	33
Chapter 4 Do I Know Truth?	47
Chapter 5 What Is Truth?	69
Chapter 6 Am I?	81
Chapter 7 I Am?	87
Chapter 8 Conscious?	155
Chapter 9 Miraculous?	241
Chapter 10 No Worries?	309

About the Author

Notice to Reader:

The publisher and author of this book accept no responsibility for the results relating to its content. The publisher and author urge all readers to employ the content of this book only in a loving, responsible and lawful manner.

Dear Reader,

This book solely contains questions. Ponder them. Savour them.

Most of the actual content of this book is not found on its pages. The content is found in your contemplation of the questions and the empty space between them, and hence within and through you. Each question leads to the next, and these together can provide a glimpse of the awesome reality that awaits your conscious recognition beyond the surface of usual and, all too often, illusory existence. Take your time. Use your sense. Stick to the truth. And feel free to always ask more questions.

May wonder ever spread throughout your consciousness, and from you, throughout our world.

Enjoy being wonder-full.

Chapter 1 WHAT IS?

What is?

What isn't?

Is 'what is' truth?

Is 'what isn't' truth?

Does 'what is' exist?

Does 'what isn't' exist?

Is reality, what is?

Is reality, what isn't?

Is reality what exists?

Is reality what doesn't exist?

Is reality truth?

Is reality not truth?

Does truth exist?

Does no truth exist?

What is truth?

Chapter 2 TRUTH?

What exists?

What does not exist?

Does everything exist?

Does nothing exist?

Does anything exist?

Does something exist?

Can I know what exists?

Can I know what doesn't exist?

How do I know what exists?

How do I know what doesn't exist?

Do I have ability to sense?

Can I see, touch, hear, smell or taste?

Do I have sense-ability?

Am I sense-able?

What happens

if I lose all my good sense?

What is my good sense?

Can I sense what exists?

Can I sense what doesn't exist?

Can I see, touch, hear, smell or taste what exists?

Can I see, touch, hear, smell or taste

what doesn't exist?

Do my senses provide me

with an awareness of what exists?

How other than via my senses

do I become aware of what exists?

Do my senses provide me

with awareness of reality?

How other than via my senses

do I become aware of reality?

Is reality truth?

Is reality not truth?

Do my senses provide me

with awareness of truth?

How other than via my senses

do I become aware of truth?

Do I sense truth?

Do I not sense truth?

Is my sense of reality

my sense of truth?

Is my sense of reality

not my sense of truth?

Is truth complicated?

Is truth uncomplicated?

What is complicated?

What is uncomplicated?

Is truth simple?

Is truth not simple?

What is simple?

What is not simple?

What is truth?

Chapter 3 DO I EXPERIENCE TRUTH?

Can I find facts?

Can I not find facts?

What are facts?

What are not facts?

Are facts truths that I and others verify using our senses?

Are facts not evidence?

Can I see a flower, touch a flower,

hear, smell, or taste a flower?

Do my senses inform me

of those facts about a flower?

Are facts evidence of reality?

Are facts not evidence of reality?

Does reality verify truth?

Does reality not verify truth?

Can I verify truth regarding how a flower looks, feels, sounds, smells or tastes?

Do I personally experience those facts about a flower?

Do I not personally experience those facts about a flower?

If I experience facts about a flower, do I know those facts?

If I know those facts about a flower,

do I then know a flower is fact?

If I know a flower is fact,

do I then know a flower is reality?

If I know a flower is reality,

do I then know a flower is truth?

Do I personally experience reality?

Do I not personally experience reality?

Do I personally experience truth?

Do I not personally experience truth?

'What is truth?

Chapter 4 DO I KNOW TRUTH?

What is experience?

What is no experience?

What is an experience?

What is not an experience?

Can I have an experience

other than via my senses?

How could I have an experience

without my senses?

Must reality be sensed

to be experienced?

Must reality be experienced

to be known?

Must truth be sensed

to be experienced?

Must truth be experienced

to be known?

Can I experience what I cannot sense?

Can I know

what I cannot experience?

How could I know

what I cannot experience?

Is truth experienced via my senses?

Is sensing something

having an experience of it?

Is sensing having an experience?

Is sensing, experience?

Is having an experience of something,

knowing it?

Is experience, knowing?

Must I know something for it to exist?

If I don't know something exists, does it still exist?

Does my knowing have any bearing on something's existence?

How can I be aware

of something's existence?

How can I not be aware

of something's existence?

When do I become aware

of something's existence?

Can I become aware of

something's existence anytime I like?

Can I not become aware of something's existence anytime I like?

Must I know how or why something exists?

If I don't know how or why something exists, can I still know it exists?

If I don't know how or why a flower exists, do I still know a flower exists by simply sensing it?

Do I know of my own existence?

Do I not know of my own existence?

If I don't know how or why I exist,

can I still know I exist?

If I don't know how or why I exist,

do I still know I exist by simply

sensing myself?

Do I know truth?

Do I not know truth?

If I don't know how or why truth exists, can I still know truth exists?

If I don't know how or why truth exists, do I still know truth exists by simply sensing?

What is truth?

Chapter 5 WHAT IS TRUTH?

Is there evidence of truth?

Is there no evidence of truth?

Is truth evidence?

Is truth not evidence?

Is truth verifiable?

Is truth unverifiable?

Can truth be sensed?

Can truth not be sensed?

Is truth fact?

Is truth not fact?

Does truth exist?

Does no truth exist?

Is 'what exists', reality?

Is 'what does not exist', reality?

Is reality truth?

Is reality not truth?

Is truth what is?

Is truth not what is?

What is?

What isn't?

What is truth?

Chapter 6 AM I?

Do I exist?

Do I not exist?

Am I reality?

Am I not reality?

Am I what is?

Am I not what is?

Am I truth?

Am I not truth?

Am I?

What is truth?

Chapter 7 I AM?

Do I seek truth?

Do I not seek truth?

How do I seek truth?

How do I not seek truth?

Why seek truth?

Why not seek truth?

How long must I seek truth?

Can I seek truth for as long

or as little as I want?

How long until I know truth?

Will it take long to know truth?

Will it not take long to know truth?

Does seeking truth alter truth?

Does not seeking truth alter truth?

Is seeking truth, seeking myself?

Is seeking ~~truth~~ not seeking myself?

Is seeking, sensing?

Can I stop sensing?

Can I stop sensing truth?

Can I stop sensing myself?

How could I stop sensing truth?

How could I stop sensing myself?

Why would I stop sensing truth?

Why would I stop sensing myself?

Do I want truth?

Do I not want truth?

Do I want myself?

Do I not want myself?

Can I handle truth?

Can I not handle truth?

Can I handle myself?

Can I not handle myself?

Can I live with truth?

Can I not live with truth?

Can I live with myself?

Can I not live with myself?

Do i live with truth?

Do I not live with truth?

Do I live with myself?

Do I not live with myself?

Do I avoid truth?

Do I not avoid truth?

Do I avoid myself?

Do I not avoid myself?

How do I avoid truth?

How do I not avoid truth?

How do I avoid myself?

How do I not avoid myself?

Why would I avoid truth?

Why would I not avoid truth?

Why would I avoid myself?

Why would I not avoid myself?

To know truth, must I know facts?

To know truth, must I know myself?

To know facts, must I have a direct experience of those facts?

To know myself, must I have a direct experience of myself?

To have a direct experience of myself, must I be honest with myself?

Is having a direct experience of facts,

honestly observing those facts?

To be honest with myself,

do I truly experience myself?

To know facts about a flower, must I have a direct experience of those facts about a flower?

If I directly experience facts about a flower, do I experience a flower?

If I experience a flower,

do I know a flower is truth?

To know facts about myself,

must I have a direct experience of

facts about myself?

If I directly experience facts about myself, do I experience myself?

If I truly experience myself, do I know myself as truth?

If I experience myself,

do I know I am truth?

If I know I am truth,

have I experienced truth?

Is truth what exists?

Is truth only what exists?

Do I exist?

Do I not exist?

Am I truth?

Am I not truth?

If I exist... if I am... am I directly experiencing truth?

If I am, am I truth?

How am I?

How am I not?

If I only experience truth,
and I am also truth, and truth is all
that is, am I, in a curious way, one
with what exists?

Can I see, touch, hear, smell, or taste
what exists?

Is what exists, the entire Universe?

Is it truth that I am, in a curious way, one with the Universe?

Is it truth that being one with the Universe, I am, in a curious way, one and the same as the Universe?

In a curious way, am I the Universe?

Am I?

Is being the Universe

difficult to comprehend?

Is being the Universe

not difficult to comprehend?

Why is being the Universe

difficult to comprehend?

Why is being the Universe

not difficult to comprehend?

Can I see, touch, hear, smell, or taste

the Universe?

Can I see, touch, hear, smell, or taste myself?

Is thought involved in sensing?

Is no thought involved in sensing?

Do I think that sensing

involves thought?

Do I think that

understanding involves thought?

Do I think that

knowing involves thought?

Does sensing involve thought?

Does understanding involve thought?

Does knowing involve thought?

Does sensing involve knowing?

Does understanding involve knowing?

Is knowing based on personal experience?

Does thinking involve knowing?

Does thinking imply not knowing?

Would I rather think I know,

or truly know?

How do I know without thinking?

Do I know simply by sensing?

Is sensing, experience?

Is there any thinking involved in sensing?

Is there no thought involved in sensing?

Does thinking actually get

in the way of sensing?

Can I sense when I am thinking?

Can I think when I am sensing?

Is there any thought involved in knowing?

Is there no thought

involved in knowing?

Is there any need

for thought when I know?

Is there no need for thought when I know?

Does thinking actually get in the way of my ability to perform?

Is it actually pointless to think when I know what to do based on my experience?

Is it not a welcome relief when I know what to do, or how to do it, and don't have to think about it?

Is that not the benefit of experience?

Do I sense the Universe?

Is my sensing the Universe,

understanding the Universe?

Is my understanding the Universe,

knowing the Universe?

Is there any point in thinking about the Universe if I can only know it by sensing it?

Does my thinking about the Universe actually get in the way of my knowing the Universe?

If I sense the Universe, and therefore

know the Universe, and I sense

myself, and therefore know myself,

am I and the Universe,

in a curious way, one?

Am I the Universe?

Am I not the Universe?

Am I?

Do I know?

How do I know?

Do I sense?

Do I not sense?

What is truth?

Chapter 8 CONSCIOUS?

Is the Universe all there is?

Is the Universe not all there is?

Is there anything

beyond the Universe?

Is nothing beyond the Universe?

How could anything be

beyond the Universe?

Can something be beyond the

Universe by underlying the Universe?

Does something

underlie the Universe?

What underlies the Universe?

Does a consciousness

that senses the Universe,

underlie the Universe?

Does the Universe exist

without a consciousness to sense it?

If there is nothing which sees, touches, hears, smells or tastes the Universe, does the Universe exist?

Whose consciousness senses the Universe?

Do I sense?

Does my consciousness grow via my sense ability?

Does my consciousness

sense the Universe?

Am I existing and growing

within the Universe?

If I sense something's existence,

does it exist?

If I don't sense something's existence,

does it exist?

Does the Universe exist?

Do I know the Universe exists?

How do I know the Universe exists?

Do I sense anything but endless facts proving the existence of the Universe?

Do I sense anything but endless facts proving my own existence?

Am I of the Universe?

Are I and the Universe

intimately connected?

How could I be separate

from the Universe?

Where do I exist

other than in the Universe?

If I exist in the Universe, am of the

Universe, and cannot be separate

from the Universe, am I and the

Universe, in a curious way,

the same thing?

Am I and the Universe, one?

Am I the Universe?

Am I not the Universe?

Is the Universe me?

Is the Universe not me?

Is the Universe conscious?

Is the Universe not conscious?

What is conscious?

What is unconscious?

What is consciousness?

What is unconsciousness?

Is consciousness, awareness?

Is unconsciousness, lack of awareness?

How could the Universe be conscious?

How could the Universe

be unconscious?

Can the Universe be

conscious through me?

Can the Universe be

unconscious through me?

Am I the Universe's consciousness?

Am I the Universe's unconsciousness?

Is my consciousness, to whatever extent I possess it, in a curious way, a universal consciousness?

Am I actually

universal consciousness?

Do I experience

universal consciousness?

How could I experience

universal consciousness?

Could I experience universal

consciousness actually quite simply?

Do I experience consciousness simply by sensing?

Do I experience universal consciousness also simply by sensing?

How other than via my senses

can I experience anything?

Does thinking provide me

with experience of anything?

Does thinking actually

get in my way of experiencing?

How other than via sensing

can the Universe experience

anything?

Is sense ability synonymous with life?

Does sense ability allow me

to respond to my environment?

Does all life respond to its environment?

What is life?

What is environment?

Can something that is not alive,

sense its environment?

Can life sense?

Can only life sense?

Is life sense-able?

Am I alive?

Am I life?

Am I sensible?

Can I sense my environment?

Can a life live but not fully sense?

How could a life live

but not fully sense?

Why would a life live

but not fully sense?

Can a life live but not fully sense

because it is damaged in some way?

Can a life that is damaged

in some way still fully sense

within its ability?

Can a life live but not fully sense

because it is simply not fully aware

of its ability to sense?

Is a life that has full sense ability,

but does not fully sense, fully alive?

Is a life that is not fully alive

unconscious?

Do I fully sense?

Do I not fully sense?

Does a life that is unconscious

fully exist?

Does a life that is unconscious exist only to the level of its unconsciousness?

Does my sensing provide me with awareness that both I and the Universe exist?

Do I fully know that I

and the Universe exist?

Are I and the Universe fully alive?

Are I and the Universe, conscious?

Are I and the Universe, life?

Am I and the Universe,

in a curious way, actually one life?

Is my knowing

the Universe's knowing?

Is my knowing, universal knowing?

Is my knowing, consciousness?

Is my thinking, knowing?

Is my thinking, not knowing?

Is my thinking, consciousness?

Is my thinking, unconscious?

Do I think I know how and

why the Universe exists?

Do I think I know how and

why I exist?

How could my thinking

know how and why

the Universe and I exist?

Must I know how and why

the Universe exists to know it exists?

Must I know how and why

I exist, to know I exist?

Must I know how and why

I exist, to exist?

Do I think the Universe exists?

Do I know the Universe exists?

Do I think I exist?

Do I know I exist?

Do I think the Universe is alive?

Do I know the Universe is alive?

Do I think I am alive?

Do I know I am alive?

Must I know how and

why the Universe lives

to know the Universe is alive?

Must I know how and

why I live to know I am alive?

Can I prove with endless facts

how and why

the Universe exists and is alive?

Can anyone prove with endless facts

how and why the Universe exists

and is alive?

Can I prove with endless facts

how and why I exist and am alive?

Can anyone prove with endless facts

how and why they exist

and are alive?

Do I know the Universe exists?

Do I not know the Universe exists?

How do I know the Universe exists?

How do I know I exist?

If I can't prove how or why the

Universe exists, but I know it exists

because I sense it, is it reasonable to

say the Universe was,

in some curious way, created?

Do I think I know how and

why and when the Universe was

created?

Can I prove with endless facts

how and why and when

the Universe was created?

Can anyone prove with endless facts

how and why and when the Universe

was created?

How could anyone even begin to

know how and why and when

the Universe was created?

Why would anyone need to know

how or why or when

the Universe was created?

Do I need to know how or why or when the Universe was created in order to enjoy life?

Can I actually enjoy life more by admitting that I have no idea how or why or when the Universe was created?

Can I actually finally enjoy life by becoming conscious of the fact that no one is ever going to honestly and definitively know how or why or when the Universe was created?

Am I enjoying life?

Am I not enjoying life?

Do I want to enjoy life?

Do I not want to enjoy life?

How do I enjoy life?

How do I not enjoy life?

Do I cling to improvable notions

of how and why and when

the Universe was created?

Was I created?

Do I know how and why and when I was created?

Can anyone prove with endless facts

how and why and when

they were ultimately created?

Will anyone ever be able to prove

with endless facts how and why and

when they were ultimately created?

Do I think I need an explanation

for how and why and when

I was ultimately created?

Why do I think I need an

explanation for how and why and

when I was ultimately created?

Can I enjoy life despite honestly

not knowing how or why or when

I was ultimately created?

Can I finally enjoy life

by admitting I do not honestly know

how or why or when

I was ultimately created?

When I live consciously knowing that

neither I nor anyone can ever

ultimately know how or why or

when I was created, do I live in a

constant state of wonder?

Is being in a state of wonder,

being full of wonder?

Is being full of wonder, wonder-full?

Is life wonderful?

Is life not wonderful?

Am I wonderful?

Am I not wonderful?

Is there, frankly, an incomprehensible explanation for the existence of everything that exists?

Do I think that?

Do I not think that?

Do I know that?

Do I not know that?

Despite the incomprehensible

reality of existence,

is my existence reality?

Is my existence not reality?

Is my existence truth?

Is my existence not truth?

Do I exist?

Do I not exist?

Am I reality?

Am I not reality?

Am I truth?

Am I not truth?

What is truth?

Chapter 9 MIRACULOUS?

Did I create myself?

Did I not create myself?

Did my parents create me?

Did my parents not ultimately create me either?

If I exist, but I did not create myself,

and neither did my parents,

how ultimately did I come into

existence?

Do I think I know

how I came into existence?

Is thinking, knowing?

Is knowing, thinking?

Do I honestly have no solid evidence

for how I was ultimately created

or actually exist?

Does that excite me or scare me?

But how did I ultimately

come into existence?

Is it undeniable, due to the fact of my

very existence, that I was, in some

curious, inexplicable way, created?

Or was I, on the other hand,

not created?

If I was not created,

what other mechanism

could account for my existence?

If I am the culmination of some process of evolution over eons of time, where did the beginnings and building blocks of that process come from?

Is it not reasonable to point out that in the mists of the distant past, even if evolution is true, there was also an unexplained start to that process from which everything that exists today must have arisen?

How is that possible?

How is that not possible?

If I am honest with myself, can I become conscious that I somehow came into existence through means that are, frankly, beyond explanation, and beyond comprehension?

Is my existence rather mind-boggling?

Do I nevertheless continue to exist?

Does thinking I can explain my existence take away from my conscious experience and enjoyment of the wonder of life?

How is it possible that I exist

but do not honestly know how or

why that is so?

Do I find that exhilarating?

Do I find that disturbing?

Do I find it even

somewhat frightening?

Is the frightening aspect of unexplained existence the reason people believe improvable stories and theories to explain existence?

Since I have no provable explanation for my existence, and apparently never will, can my existence honestly be described in any way other than miraculous?

Is existence miraculous?

Is existence not miraculous?

Is my personal existence miraculous?

Is my personal existence

not miraculous?

What is miraculous?

What is not miraculous?

What is a miracle?

What is not a miracle?

Is a miracle an unexplained wonderful occurrence of immense magnitude?

Am I an unexplained wonderful occurrence of immense magnitude?

Do miracles occur?

Do no miracles occur?

Do I think miracles occur?

Do I think no miracles occur?

Do I know miracles occur?

Do I know miracles do not occur?

Do I think miracles occur in my life?

Do I think miracles

do not occur in my life?

Do I know miracles occur in my life?

Do I know miracles do not occur in my life?

Is life a miracle?

Is life not a miracle?

Is all life a miracle?

Is all life not a miracle?

Am I a miracle?

Am I not a miracle?

If I accept the fact that life and my existence is miraculous, how do I handle that truth?

If life and my existence is miraculous, how do I not handle that truth?

Do I contemplate

the miracle of my existence?

Do I never contemplate

the miracle of my existence?

What would happen if I spent more time contemplating the miracle of my existence?

What would not happen if I spent more time contemplating the miracle of my existence?

Was every bit of me

somehow created miraculously?

Was any part of me

somehow not created miraculously?

If my miraculous creation is reality,

is miraculous creation truth?

Is miraculous creation truth?

Is miraculous creation not truth?

Am I intimately and utterly

connected with miraculous creation?

Am I not intimately and utterly connected with miraculous creation?

Are I and miraculous creation, truth?

Am I and miraculous creation

ultimately the same thing?

Am I creation?

Do I create?

Do I destroy?

Do I create to live?

Do I destroy to live?

If I create, am I truly living?

If I destroy, am I truly living?

If every bit of me, as well as the entire Universe, was miraculously created, how could I be other than one with creation, all that exists, the Universe, and the universal consciousness of creation?

How could I, a walking miracle, be separate from and exist outside of what miraculously exists?

Can anything real

be separate from what exists?

Is what exists only what is real?

Is everything real, miraculous?

Is what is real, truth?

Is what is not real, truth?

If I am one with miraculous creation, and I am conscious, do I actually experience the miraculous consciousness of creation?

Am I the miraculous

consciousness of creation?

Am I?

What is the consciousness of creation?

What is not

the consciousness of creation?

How do I know

the consciousness of creation?

How can I not know

the consciousness of creation?

Do I have sense?

Do I have no sense?

Can I sense when I am distracted?

Can I sense best

when I am undistracted?

Where and when am I distracted?

Where and when am I undistracted?

What distracts me?

What does not distract me?

When I sense, am I conscious?

When I don't sense, am I unconscious?

When I am distracted, do I sense?

When I am undistracted, do I sense?

When I am distracted,

do I sense the miraculous

consciousness of creation?

When I am undistracted,

do I sense the miraculous

consciousness of creation?

Is the miraculous consciousness

of creation, my consciousness?

Is that everyone's consciousness?

Is that simply what consciousness is?

Is consciousness a special ability?

Is consciousness nothing special?

Is consciousness miraculous?

Is consciousness not miraculous?

Is consciousness synonymous with life?

Is consciousness not synonymous with life?

If I'm not aware that consciousness is life, am I fully conscious?

If I'm not aware that consciousness is miraculous, am I fully conscious?

Am I intimately connected to everything that exists through an inexplicably miraculous universal consciousness?

Are all things connected?

Am I connected to everything?

Does this connection explain synchronicity, serendipity, and coincidence?

Do such events seem ridiculous?

Do such events seem miraculous?

Can I ever be separate

from everything?

Can i never be separate

from everything?

Am I everything?

Am I not everything?

How do I know what is truth?

How do I know truth?

Can I sense?

Can I not sense?

Do I sense?

Do I not sense?

Does truth make sense to me?

Does truth make no sense to me?

What is truth?

Chapter 10 NO WORRIES?

What is not truth?

Does 'what is not truth' exist?

Is the 'what is not truth' that presents itself as truth, illusion?

What is illusion?

What is not illusion?

Does illusion exist?

Does illusion not exist?

Does illusion masquerade as truth?

Is a masquerade of truth,

illusion's existence?

How does illusion exist?

How does illusion not exist?

How can illusion exist?

How can illusion not exist?

Why does illusion exist?

Why does illusion not exist?

How do I detect illusion?

How do I not detect illusion?

Can I see, touch, hear, smell or taste illusion?

Can I see, touch, hear, smell or taste truth?

Can I dig as deep as I like into truth and endlessly find only more facts that prove truth?

Can I dig into illusion and quickly and easily dispel illusion by seeking proof but finding none?

Does illusion avoid inspection?

Do illusionists conceal the truth behind their tricks?

Does truth invite scrutiny?

Can truth withstand all scrutiny?

Does truth hide nothing?

Is illusion easily unmasked by truth?

Does illusion disappear instantly in the face of truth?

Does truth wear no mask?

Is truth forever open, honest, real, solid, deep, unwavering, indestructible, exciting and reliable?

Is illusion a pathetic facsimile of truth, shallow, two-dimensional, deceitful, boring and unreliable?

Is something reliable, good?

Is something unreliable, bad?

Is truth good?

Is illusion bad?

Would I rather build my life

on unreliable illusion,

or unassailable truth?

If I have children,

which would they prefer I build

my and their lives on?

Do I rely on illusion?

Do I rely on truth?

Do I live with illusion?

Do I live with truth?

Can I live with illusion?

Can I live with truth?

Do I live with what is, what exists, reality, truth?

Do I only live with what is,

what exists, reality, truth,

whether I know it or not, anyway?

Was I conscious of that fact?

Was I not conscious of that fact?

Would it be best for me
to wake up to that fact?

Would it be best if I did

not wake up to that fact?

How do I live with

what is, what exists, reality, truth?

How do I not live with

what is, what exists, reality, truth?

How is my life

if I live within an illusion?

How is my life if I do not live within an illusion?

How is my life if I live with truth?

How is my life

if I do not live with truth?

How will my life change

if I live with truth?

How will my life not change

if I live with truth?

How will my life change

if I live with illusion?

How will my life not change

if I live with illusion?

If I'm dealing with truth,

what am I dealing with?

If I'm living with truth,

am I dealing with what exists?

If I'm living with truth,

am I dealing with what doesn't exist?

If I'm not dealing with truth,

what am I dealing with?

Why would I worry about what

doesn't exist?

What is truth?

About the Author:

Darren J Nast lives on beautiful Vancouver Island, British Columbia, Canada. Darren has contemplated life while engaged in study, business, travel, writing, music, photography, beachcombing, hiking, kayaking, mountain biking, communication, relationships, family and parenting. Darren is awed and humbled by existence. He hopes to meet you one day.

Ponder a Paradox Publishing
Victoria, B.C.
CANADA

Our Mission:

Foster global awareness of miraculous existence.

Order additional copies of this book and other Ponder a Paradox Publishing publications on Amazon.com.

For more info visit:
www.ponderaparadox.com

www.ingramcontent.com/pod-product-compliance
Lightning Source LLC
LaVergne TN
LVHW051541070426
835507LV00021B/2358